Words of the Mind

Emily Heneisen

Presentation by *BookLeaf Publishing*

Web: www.bookleafpub.com

E-mail: info@bookleafpub.com

ISBN: 9789358315141

First edition 2023

*To the six inches between your ears, and to
the man who taught me to master mine.
Thanks, Coach.*

The Patient

There are monsters in my house.
I cannot leave my room.
I don't know how long I've been here.
I feel a sense of doom.

They open my door every morning.
They bring trays of water and food.
Sleek, white monsters in surgical masks
Their auras hold a heavy mood.
Heavy mood.

They check the covers on my walls.
They assess my skin and bones.
They look deep into my watery eyes,
Searching for a soul neither of us owns.
No soul for either of us.
Nowhere.

Sometimes, they stick a needle
Into the fleshy side of my arm.
I kick and scream but they persist.
I cannot tell how badly they harm.
Harm.
I did not hurt that boy, I swear.
Why am I here?

They tell me I killed someone,
That I committed a horrible crime.
I cannot remember my past,
And I cannot fill the slots of missing time.
I did not kill the boy.
Wait, did I?
Yes, I did. His body is in the river.
But I won't tell the monsters that, no.
They would be upset and stick
Another pointy thing in my arm
And then I would be angry and
I do not like to be angry because
Then I do bad things.

The monsters keep me trapped.
I cannot leave my room.
If I confess, I'm ruined.
If I stay silent, I'm doomed.

The Tulip

I was young when I acquired it,
The tiny, tulip seed.
It was small and fragile,
Filled with want and need.

I took it to my little garden,
I prepared the earth with care.
I tucked the seed into rich soil.
I gave it light and fresh air.

I tended to the small, sweet seed.
I helped it to grow and sprout.
I watered it every single day.
I watched its leaves stretch out.

For weeks I nurtured and loved
My precious little tulip seed.
He grew and flourished and bloomed.
He was everything I could want or need.

Then, one stormy, dreadful day
Sometime towards the end of July
I came to the little garden
And let out a horrible cry.

My sweet, baby flower was gone.
His petals were withered and shriveled and cold.
His leaves were brown and dry.
It was a tragic, awful sight to behold.

By now, I hope you've realized.
I have never found a flower.
I do not have a garden,
But my heart is still sour.

It was not a tulip that I lost,
But they make me sad to see.
I lost my son that stormy July.
Of the grief, I wish to be free.

The Traveler

I like to go to the bluest oceans.
I swim to the deepest depths.
The fish and crabs are friends.
I never run out of breath
I'm weightless underwater.

I've seen calm, peaceful meadows.
I make crowns from the wildflowers.
I have picnics in the green grove.
The ancient willow tree towers
Over me as I nap in the shade.

Sometimes I dance on rainbows.
My head can reach the clouds.
I twirl among the stars above.
I go as high as my mind allows,
And I know I'll never fall down.

Sometimes I can't control it,
The withdrawn look in my eyes
As I sit with people around the table,
Hearing their laughs and their cries
But they're muffled and muted.

As they speak of politics,

Of anger and hate and wars,
I climb the tallest mountains.
I sail to the warmest shores.
I fly through fluffy, white clouds.

When the world around me
Is boring, sad, or dull,
I sink beneath sweet waves
In my mind and feel the lull
Of the ocean as my senses fade.

The Mirror

There is a man I see often.
Every morning and every night.
He's part of my routine now.
He makes my day feel right.

He's a man of great beauty.
His eyes are deep blue.
His hair is like the finest silk.
His clothes are always new.

He's a very smart man,
More intelligent than most.
He's very rarely wrong.
Though, he doesn't like to boast.

He has a lot of friends,
But they're not quite as great.
They don't have his looks or smarts.
There is not much debate.

He can get any girl he wants.
He takes many beauties to dinner.
Even with the prettiest woman,
He always leaves a winner.

He's the biggest, brightest star
On a clear, summer night.
In a castle full of peasants,
He's a gracious, noble knight.

No. That was incorrect.
He would be the benevolent king.
He could fight all wars.
He could solve anything.

I see this brilliant man
Every morning, every day.
He looks right back at me,
My reflection on display.

The Shadow

Getting out of bed
Is quite difficult these days.
I lie awake and silent.
I contemplate the ways
I could've ended up here.

There's a shadow that I know.
He lives inside my head.
I wish that he'd come out
And go away instead.
I don't know why he's here.

My shadow first appeared
Not too long ago.
He started small at first,
But he's only seemed to grow
Until there was no more room.

He's quite a large shadow now.
He feels quite cramped in my mind.
There's hardly room for other things,
And I can barely seem to find
Time for things I used to enjoy.

My shadow makes me sad sometimes.

He makes me feel alone.
I never go outside anymore.
I barely touch my phone.
Perhaps my friends have forgotten me.

That might be for the best.
My shadow wouldn't want
For me to be around others,
And I do look sort of gaunt.
Maybe more sleep will help.

Except, I know it won't.
My shadow invades my dreams,
And he brings darkness with him.
Even now it seems
Like he'll never let me go.

I want to get out of bed today,
I want to do something good.
But my shadow weighs me down
Just like I knew he would.
I guess I'll just stay home today.

The Bomb

Have you ever lit a fuse before?
I have.
I've seen the rope across the floor.

Have you ever watched the spark ignite?
I have.
I watched as it blazed with light.

The thing about a bomb is this:
Once it's lit, it starts to fizz.
It sizzles down the winding rope.
Best if you go ahead and lose hope.
The fire won't stop until KABOOM!
And everything around it is doomed.
So once you light the fuse, my friend.
The ticking bomb will be your end.

My brain is like that bomb right now.
Time itself seems to slow down
As I move in slow motion towards the bomb.
The crackling fuse is an inch from my palm.
But I can't reach it in time, I know I won't.
I want to stomp out the flame but I don't.
The world moves so fast these days, I know.
I'm falling behind, I'm running too slow.

The marathon that I'm desperate to win
Will be my biggest success or my worst sin.
Because if I can't complete this one task,
Then I'll have to remove my perfect mask.
And if people see the man underneath
Do you think they'll continue to accept me?

I'm running, running, running, then boom.
The bomb goes off and it's over too soon.

There's something caught in my throat,
I can't breath, can't even croak.
My heart is racing, still in the marathon,
But it's over and done with, the prize is gone.
My head is spinning, my vision's a blur.
I wish things would go back to the way they
were.

Before the bomb, before the fuse,
Before I was terrified to lose.
Before the pressure built this high.
Before my heart rate hit the sky.
Before the never-ending run.
Back when I had always won.

The Pianist

This measure hurts the most.
I must play the notes.
One, two, three.
G, G#, C#.

I have to get it right.
I cannot fail tonight.
One, two, three.
G, G#, C#.

Almost done now,
No mistakes allowed.
One, two, three.
G, G#, C.

Wait, that wasn't right.
That was a wrong note.
One, two, three.
G, G#, C#.

Dammit, did anyone see?
No, it's only the piano and me.
One, two, three.
G, G#, C#.

The practice room is hot.
My tired fingers are shot.
One, two, three.
G, G#, C.

Dammit, I lost focus, and then
My fingers slipped again.
One, two, three.
G, G#...

No, it's too late now.
I'm not quite sure how,
But I've failed the song
And I can't just trudge along.
I have to restart,
I have to get it right.
I don't care
If it takes me all night

One, two, three.
G, G#, C#.
One, two, three.
G, G#, C#.

The Siren

In waters deep, a siren's song plays,
An alluring dance, a deadly price to pay.
A witch cloaked in veils of pretty deceit,
Her cruel embrace is binding and concrete.

Beneath the moon's soft and seductive light,
She sings with a promise, cold and bright,
Her eyes, like embers, burn with fiery greed,
As in her clutches, many hearts she'll feed.

She sings a tune of sweet ecstasy,
A fleeting high that drowns reality,
Her notes are a symphony of false delight,
That draws my soul into the endless night.

I chase her call, believing I'd be set free,
But I am her prisoner, lost in misery,
And in her clutches, I may meet my end.
Into my love for a temptress, I descend.

I wade through waters dense with lies,
Where the current of craving never dies.
My limbs burrow deep in rough sand,
As innocence succumbs to pain's demand.

The taste of poison, like a honeyed wine,
The sweet allure is a trap, a grand design.
A prisoner to the longing, to my own chain,
A willing captive to the siren's bane.

But hope still flickers, like a distant star,
In hearts that bear the siren's heavy scar.
For in the darkest depths, the light may gleam,
Redemption's whisper, like a silent dream.

To break the chains– to heal and to be free,
Takes a distance swim. I'll wade endlessly.
In strength and love, I find the will to fight,
To conquer the siren, to reclaim my light.

The Pendulum

I live in a realm of emotions, wild and free,
It's a rollercoaster ride, a violent storm at sea,
A pendulum that swings, relentless and severe,
From elation's peak to the shadow's eerie sneer.

The flip of a coin, a watchful moon's control,
Between the highs of mania, and the depths of a
soul,
A tempestuous journey through a turbulent
night,
Where my mind's light and shadow endlessly
fight.

At the top, the world's a canvas painted bright,
A symphony of colors, a celestial flight,
My mind is a rocket soaring high above,
In the euphoria, the heart knows only love.

But then the descent, a plummet to the abyss,
The bottom of a cavern where darkness finds its
kiss,
The once-vibrant rainbow now fades to gray,
In the very heart of gloom's cold dismay.

Now, I'm back again in the sun's dazzling light,

My joyous fever bursting to new heights.
My heart is a fiery dance of passion and desire.
Yet even the stars burn out, and so I tire.

The night descends with a heavy cloak.
Misery's weight like thick, invading smoke.
A silent void, a never-ending, obsidian sea
Where shadows linger and want to be free.

The Voices

Do you hear the voices
Outside the door?
Their whispers and hisses
Chill me to the core.

I hear their footsteps,
On the other side of the wood.
They speak in an alien tongue.
I wish I understood.

I opened the door once,
Back when they first appeared.
There was no one there
But the air in the hall felt weird.

I haven't touched the door since then.
I haven't made a sound.
It's been days, maybe weeks.
The voices keep coming around.

Sometimes, they'll leave,
For maybe an hour or so.
But they always return to my door,
Their whispers eerie and slow.

Can you hear them, too?
Or are they only in my mind?
Is it just my imagination?
Behind the door, what will I find?

The Shards

The body is a canvas, a work of art,
But your thoughts tear it up, piece by part.
A whirlwind of words, a storm in the mind,
Twisting and turning, a merciless bind.

This glass, a portal to your fractured mind,
Where love made of shards is hard to find,
A fragile image, marred by your doubt and fear,
The mirror's truth, your heart cannot adhere.

In the distorted glass, flaws are magnified,
The image warped, your beauty set aside,
Each imperfection etched in stark relief,
A painful untruth, a never-ending grief.

Your cruel, endless hunger that never abates,
A voracious beast, insatiable, it waits.
Chasing a beauty that's fleeting and thin,
It's never enough; no one can ever win.

Beneath the surface, the chaos takes hold,
Like a wildfire raging, relentless, and bold.
It masquerades as control, a deceptive guise,
But it's a prison of torment, a web of lies.

Whispers in the darkness, a siren's call,
Your hunger for perfection, a relentless thrall.
But the cost is too high, the toll too immense,
As life's colors fade, joy is your expense.

What you see in the mirror is a false illusion.
Your self-image shatters in the delusion.
Beneath the surface is a warring sea,
Where your emotions are in misery.

The Labyrinth

In the labyrinth of memory, I roam,
Through misty corridors, no place is home.
The threads of thought unravel day by day,
A tapestry of time that slowly fades away.

Each morning, I awaken to the haze,
A world of strangers lost within a maze,
I search for names and faces, now unknown,
The past, like smoke, whisps away, windblown.

The clock's hands spin, but time eludes my
grasp,
Like grains of sand through fragile fingers,
clasp,
My yesterdays, like whispers in the labyrinth
wind,
A fragile thread, by fading light, is ultimately
thinned.

Familiar rooms are now strangers to my eye,
My mind loses hold of moments passing by,
A heart, once mine, now a puzzle to be solved,
A journey into darkness as the labyrinth
evolved.

The laughter, tears, the stories left unsaid,
Now fragments scattered, like a dream misled,
I turn a corner, some hope in my heart,
Yet, another dead end, the maze restarts.

As I wander through this hazy, misty zone,
In the damned labyrinth of memory, alone,
I'll hold onto hope, the lone light in the growing abyss,
For I must have somewhere a memory of bliss.

The Soldier

In shadows deep where memories reside,
A haunting specter, a pain that won't subside,
A silent scream, a wounded and tortured soul,
Invisible scars, trauma's permanent toll.

A soldier's heart, once pure, now scarred and
torn,
In visions through the night, the battles borne,
The ceaseless echoes of the guns that blaze,
The crimson rivers, in those blood-soaked days.

The flashbacks come unbidden, like a storm.
Intrusive thoughts, a nightmare will perform.
The past, a callous and unrelenting ghost,
Unleashing waves of hurt to its unwilling host.

A prisoner within one's own mind and soul,
A battle fought where none can take control.
The sleepless nights, the sweat-soaked sheets,
The silent cries for respite and peace,

My dreams thrust me back to that fateful day,
Where life and death danced in a cursed fray,
A battlefield of horrors etched in my mind,
The aftermath of chaos is cruel and unkind.

The thunderous roar of gunfire in the air,
The acrid stench of fear, a constant layer,
A platoon of terrified hearts, echoing still,
Through sleepless nights, the marching drills.

A flash of light, a sudden loud surprise,
A harsh reminder, tears in wounded eyes,
A car backfiring, or a slamming door,
Ignites the past, and I'm there once more.

A crowded street, a bustling city square,
Where laughter rings, people are unaware,
Yet, in this crowd, I stand alone, adrift,
Engulfed in solitude, my soul feels split.

The weight of guilt, of what I should have done,
Of comrades lost, their faces fade one by one,
The helplessness, the feeling of despair,
A heavy shroud, a cross I'm forced to bear.

In battle, there's a strength I've found,
A resilience deep within and profound,
Though shadows linger, darkness may persist,
I'll keep on fighting. For in my heart, they exist.

The Liar

My gaze is cold, my emotions concealed,
A distant observer, never truly revealed.
I mimic your laughter, your joy, your pain,
But deep down inside, I have nothing to gain.

My feelingless tale, a life lived in gray,
No compass guiding, no moral array.
I move through the world devoid of remorse,
A predator hunting for my dinner course.

I charm and beguile, with words that deceive,
To get what I want, to make you believe.
But behind the smile, my motives remain,
Hidden from view, a heart dark and stained.

I study your cues, your weaknesses I find,
To manipulate and control, a puppeteer's bind.
Yet, in the mirror, I see a stranger's face,
A gaping hole in my heart, a desolate space.

I've hurt and I've damaged without any regret.
Empathy is a man I've never once met.
My ungenerous world, a lonely abode,
No compassion to be found or bestowed.

But in my chest, if you should dare
To seek the humanity or glimpse the despair
Perhaps, just maybe, buried deep inside
Is a wounded spirit, a soul trying to hide.

The Garden

The whimsical Garden of the Mind,
A symphony of colors, bold and bright.
Thoughts like butterflies in chaos roam.
In all directions, they take flight.

Yet the breeze, the whirling air
Guides them on an erratic course.
It shifts and bends, unaware
That they transform with undirected force.

Each idea is a flower petal untamed.
No linear path, no predictable plot.
In the whirlwind of life, most are unnamed.
It's just a hurricane of notions and thought.

Each petal holds a fiery spark,
A fleeting thought in an ever-shifting realm.
An endless canvas of color and light
Where every bud stands at its own helm.

The mind is a playground teeming with treasures
But the speed of the elusive bird cannot be
measured.
It flits and flutters, a fleeting delight,
Chasing it feels like an endless night.

In a world where chaos blooms like wildflowers,
This garden is only the more erratic.
Despite the focus, the effort, the skill,
The garden can never be static.

And though the path may twist and turn and
twine,
Those in the Garden will always find their way.
A spark of genius in their souls will shine
And help them navigate the ever-shifting day.

The Duet

I am the laughter, the sunlight in your day,
With carefree steps, I dance and brightly sway.
In joy and sunshine, I find my way to soar,
A heart unburdened, life's pleasures I explore.

And I, the shadow, lurking in the night,
In whispered secrets, fears take flight.
With solemn gaze, I bear the weight of woes,
In quiet reflection, where the darkness grows.

I greet the dawn with hope and open eyes,
With boundless dreams that reach open skies.
Each sunrise paints a canvas fresh and bright,
A world of possibility, a thrilling flight.

While I, in the moon's embrace, seek the stars,
The quiet solitude, the night's calm memoirs.
I watch the world in shadows, where it hides,
Where introspection in the silence abides.

I love the laughter, songs of heart's delight,
In friendships woven strong, I take my flight.
With open arms, I greet each passerby,
In bonds of love and laughter, I rely.

Yet I, the introvert, in solitude's embrace,
Find solace in the stillness, in the quiet space.
In loneliness' arms, where shadows blend,
I find the depth of thoughts on which I depend.

I chase the winds and run with careless grace,
At every moment, there's a smile on my face.
With boundless energy, I'm ready to roam,
My spirit soars in search of the unknown.

But I, the thinker, walk a different path,
In silent contemplation of the world's wrath.
In thoughts and dreams, the inner world I find,
In stillness and reflection, the quiet of the mind.

Two souls within, we dance this tango true,
Different shades and colors, shifting points of
view.
With every turn, we weave a grand tapestry,
Where both of us, in our hearts, are truly free.

Two voices intertwined, a delicate duet,
In quiet and in laughter, we coexist, and yet,
We are but one, in the same vessel bound,
Two lives entwined, two different sounds.

The Bully

In a world of schoolyard laughter and games,
A boy stood silent, teased with cruel names,
Jagged wounds etched deep within his heart,
A world of isolation, his heart torn apart.

Lonely, he walked through those echoing halls,
The weight of torment on his shoulders falls,
Disguised tears, hidden behind his smile,
As bullies taunted, just to laugh for a while.

He yearned for friendship, a hand to hold,
A place to belong, a heart that wasn't cold,
But the shadows of rejection loomed large,
An outcast's path on an unsteady barge.

Each day, the laughter echoed in his ears,
The taunts, the jeers, the torment, the sneers,
He felt like a shipwreck, lost on an unending
sea,
Invisible chains, no hope or chance to break
free.

His solitude was a silent, stifling room,
A self-imposed exile, an eternal gloom,
Invisible walls, built to shield his heart,

Yet, in the process, they tore him apart.

Unseen battles fought behind closed doors,
Where the lonely boy's soul often roared,
Concealed strength, a quiet resilience,
Hidden from a world of painful indifference.

Though loneliness is a heavy burden to bear,
He carried it with grace like a silent prayer.
Beautiful dreams in the corners of his mind,
A hope that someday, acceptance he would find.

For in the heart of the lonely, there's a fire,
A spark of resilience that won't ever tire,
Invisible courage: it's what kept him strong.
As he endured, he'd prove the doubters wrong.

And in time, the world began to see,
The strength that lived in his invisibility,
No longer bound by the bullies' reign,
The lonely boy emerged unchained.

The Search

In the caverns of my home, I search in vain,
For a missing piece, a link that's slipped my
chain,
A vital, crucial item, now lost in the abyss,
My heart pounds, my thoughts caught in a twist.

The compulsion's grip tightens like a vice,
As anxiety freezes my heart in solid ice.
I trace my steps, retrace, and then again.
In this obsessive quest, my patience wanes.

Each corner turned, each cupboard explored,
My world reduced to chaos, thoughts ignored,
My mind's a housefire, my heart is ablaze,
As I hunt for what I've lost in a frenzied craze.

The ritual starts; I check, I count, I pray,
To alleviate the panic, to clear the fray,
The nagging doubt, a constant undertow,
This never-ending search, a ceaseless woe.

My hands tremble, my heart racing in my chest,
As I wrestle with this compulsive manifest,
To find that missing item, lost in the haze.
My mind is a prison, caught in a relentless maze.

Each glance, each touch, a reassurance sought,
To ease the torment, the mind's tangled thoughts.
The weight of obsession, a dark and heavy
shroud,
As I seek what's lost within this mental cloud.

Invisible bonds tie me to this quest,
A need to find it and put my mind at rest,
If I fail, a dreadful and dreary cost,
I must retrieve the item that I've lost.

Oh. I found it under the dresser here.
My nerves ease, and my mind clears.
I finally recovered the very crucial thing.
What was it, you ask? A cheap, plastic ring.

The Fires

In the depths of Jane's soul, a hurricane brews,
Uncontrollable anger, a storm she can't refuse,
A raging fire, a force she can't hope to contain,
She fears the consequences, the damage, the
pain.

Ben got caught in a cyclone of his own design,
Fury and frustration fuel him, a turbulent sign,
He dreads the moment when he might lose
control,
Unleash this demon that resides within his soul.

Lana's heart races fast, like thunder's roar,
The flames of hate ignite at her very core,
She fights to suppress the storm's rising tide,
For in its wake, she's afraid of what she'll find.

A hurricane of emotions, wild and untamed,
Innocence and reason, forever maimed,
Dan longs for peace, for a tranquil heart,
But the anger within threatens to tear him apart.

I see the fear reflected in their eyes,
For those they care for as their anger flies,
They plea from within, a battle to restrain,

The inner demons that they strive to contain.

For in the darkest moments of their lives,
They are aware of whom they deprive,
They fear the pain they might inflict on the
world,
As they struggle to control the furious whirls.

They seek the strength to quell the raging sea,
To break the chains of their angry entity,
They long for peace, for healing, and for grace,
To find a way to tame their inner space.

In this battle, they've not yet lost. I see
Support and guidance, the possibility,
To channel the fury into something good,
To find serenity in a world misunderstood.

The Cliff

Amidst the shadows, on the cliff's dark edge,
I wrestle with thoughts that dredge,
The depths of my despair, a heavy heart,
Contemplating the end, a choice to depart.

I gaze at the abyss, the chasm wide,
My life, a turbulent and raging tide,
My heart's a battlefield, a wounded soul,
Haunted by the past, which took its toll.

I walk the tightrope of life's cruel design,
I reflect on my choices, and my heart is
confined.
The mistakes that bind me, like chains of lead,
The weight of regrets, a crown of thorns on my
head.

I think of dreams I never dared to chase,
Lost in the shuffle, in life's hurried race,
The people I once hurt with words unkind,
The bridges I burned, the wreckage left behind.

I dwell on love, the ones I pushed away,
In moments of darkness, the things I'd say,
The friendships shattered, bonds forever torn,

In my quest for happiness, what hate was born?

As I stand upon that precipice of pain,
The wind howls loud, like an echoing refrain,
My heart's in turmoil, my thoughts are bleak,
Is this the end that I was destined to seek?

But in the depth of despair, a glimmer shines,
A memory of better days, those cherished times.
A love once lost, those friendships betrayed,
Are now chances to rebuild, debts to repay.

The sun sets low, casting a golden hue,
A symbol of hope in the sky's vast view,
I contemplate the value of my life,
Do I try to endure or to end this bitter strife?

I step back from the edge, my heart still sore,
I wish to seek redemption, to heal what's torn,
For in this darkest moment, I've found a way,
To face the dawn and greet a brand-new day.

The Simple

In the journey of life, there's a path we tread,
A road to recovery, where our spirits are fed,
For in the midst of struggle and moments of
despair,
We find the strength to mend and heal and
repair.

In the quiet of dawn, when the world awakes,
We find joy in the sunrise, the breeze as it
shakes,
The chorus of birds, with their songs so sweet,
Reminds us that life's treasures are a wonderful
treat.

A child's laughter, pure and unrefined,
A precious balm soothes the troubled mind,
In their innocence, they teach us to see,
The magic in moments, the unburdened glee.

The kiss of a breeze on a hot summer's day,
A moment of respite in a world that's astray,
To feel its cool touch on a sun-heated face,
Is to find joy in the simple, a moment to
embrace.

The love of a friend in a heartfelt hug,
A connection unbroken, no pulls or tugs.
The warmth of a hand in times of need,
A gesture that tells us we're heard and seen.

In the gentle flow of a tranquil stream,
A reminder that life's a beautiful dream.
With each ripple and shimmer of water so clear,
We find solace in nature, a comfort so sincere.

The scent of fresh blooms in a garden so bright,
The colors that paint the canvas of light.
In the fragrance of petals, life's beauty resides,
In the simplest of pleasures, joy coincides.

The taste of a meal shared with loved ones dear,
In the joy of conversation, the laughter is
sincere.
With each bite and each sip, we find harmony,
In the flavors of life, shared in loving company.

A starry night sky, filled with wonders untold,
Each constellation, a story of the old,
In the cosmic ballet, where galaxies play,
We find beauty in the night and dance until day.

The melody of music is a symphony in the air.
In its notes and rhythms, we find solace to bear.
A harmony of sounds, a chorus so grand,

In the music of life, we take our stand.

In recovery's journey, where the heart is set free,
We embrace each moment with a spirit of glee,
For in the little things, we find life's true art,
A collection of joy, in each beat of the heart.

So let us not forget, in our haste to the grand,
The beauty in simplicity, life's grains of sand.
For it's in the small moments where our hearts
find their song,
That the path to happiness is where we all
belong.